Chess
FOR Beginners

MICHAEL BASMAN

SECOND EDITION

DK Delhi

Senior Art Editor Ragini Rawat **Project Editor** Kathakali Banerjee
Senior Picture Researcher Sumedha Chopra
Managing Editor Kingshuk Ghoshal **Managing Art Editor** Govind Mittal
DTP Coordinator Vishal Bhatia **Hires Coordinator** Jagtar Singh
DTP Designers Pawan Kumar, Deepak Mittal **Senior Jackets Coordinator** Priyanka Sharma Saddi

DK London

Senior Editor Steven Carton
Managing Editor Rachel Fox **Managing Art Editor** Owen Peyton Jones
Senior Production Editor Andy Hilliard **Senior Production Controller** Meskerem Berhane
Jacket Designer Stephanie Cheng Hui Tan **Jacket Design Development Manager** Sophia MTT
Publisher Andrew Macintyre **Associate Publishing Director** Liz Wheeler
Art Director Karen Self **Publishing Director** Jonathan Metcalf

US Consultants Andrew Mackowiak, Andra Paitz

FIRST EDITION

Project Editor Elinor Greenwood **Senior Art Editor** Marcus James
Managing Editor Mary Ling **Managing Art Editor** Rachael Foster
Digital Artwork Robin Hunter **Photography** Steve Gorton
DTP Designer Almudena Díaz **Picture Researcher** Andrea Sadler
Jacket Designer Stephanie Cheng Hui Tan **Production** N-J Maun

This edition published in 2024
First published in Great Britain in 2001 by
Dorling Kindersley Limited
DK, One Embassy Gardens, 8 Viaduct Gardens,
London, SW11 7BW

The authorised representative in the EEA is
Dorling Kindersley Verlag GmbH. Arnulfstr. 124,
80636 Munich, Germany

ISBN 978-0-2416-5890-1

Printed and bound in China

www.dk.com

Contents

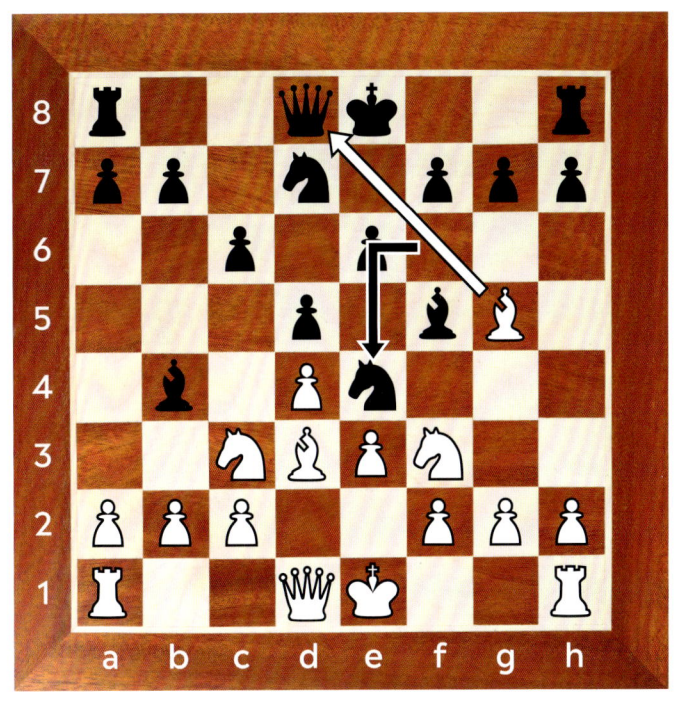

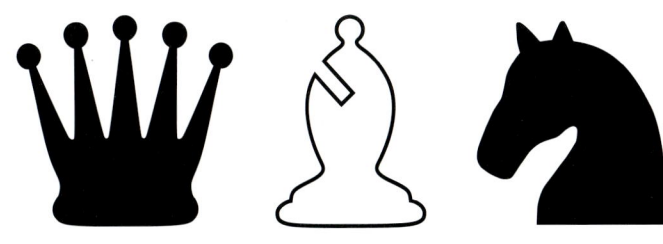

To all young chess players

All over the world people are taking up the challenge of chess, meeting new opponents, and testing their mental strength. The power of the mind – the avenue to success in business and study – is awakened, developed, and strengthened by chess. There is no feeling more satisfying than beating an able opponent, and to be a winner you just need confidence, concentration, and the ability to learn – from books, videos, computers, and your own defeats. Chess was once the game of royalty, but is now open to everyone.

I have been playing chess since I was 10 years old, and since then I haven't been away from a chess board for long! Each game I play is still exciting and challenging. Since becoming an International Master in 1981, I have devoted my time to teaching chess to school children. In 1996, I launched the UK Chess Challenge. I have made many friends through playing chess and enjoy the friendly rivalry the game encourages.

MICHAEL BASMAN

Early history

Chess has a long history. It is at least 1,500 years old. The oldest pieces that have been dug up date from the 6th century CE. Before that, chess might have been played, but no one can be sure. Chess is certainly a descendant of the Indian game Chaturanga, meaning "four sides" – because Indian armies were made up of four parts: the chariots, the cavalry, the elephants, and the footsoldiers. The ultimate war-game, chess is based on ancient battle scenarios that can still be applied to the game played by people all over the world today.

Chess goes west
The game of chess spread with the opening of markets between the Far East and Persia in the 10th century. Arab merchants plying their way along the famous Silk Road would often have a chess set among their baggage. As a result, travellers and traders eventually introduced chess into Europe.

Chinese chess
A close relation to chess is the Chinese game of *Xiàngqí* (meaning "elephant game"), which is still very popular in China. It was being played as early as the 4th century BCE.

An explosive growth in interest
Until the late 19th century, chess had earned the nickname "the game of kings" because of its popularity among the upper classes. However, in the 20th century, ordinary people started taking up the game in their thousands.

The chess set

A chess set is made up of 32 pieces and a board. The board acts as a simple battlefield, where there are no trees, rivers, hills, valleys, or buildings to hide behind. This means you can control the events of the battle far better than any army general. The pieces are the opposing armies, and the numbers on both sides are the same, so the game begins on an equal footing. It is how you move your pieces that determines eventual victory – or defeat.

Your army

Chess pieces come in many shapes and sizes. But the pieces most widely used are the Staunton-pattern pieces, which are the ones used in tournaments and in this book. The two armies are collectively called "the pieces". In your army you have a king, a queen, two bishops, two knights, two rooks, and eight pawns. (Note: some chess players think of pawns as different to "the pieces", meaning king, queen, rooks, knights, and bishops, though technically they are all "pieces".)

The battlefield

There are special terms for the rows of squares going sideways – these are called the "ranks". There are eight ranks on the chess board. The columns that go vertically, top to bottom, are called "files". There are also eight of these. Lastly, the squares of the same colour going in one direction are called "diagonals". Surprisingly enough, there are 26 diagonals on the chess board.

Files are columns that run from one player's end to the other's. Here the edge file is highlighted.

A diagonal is marked by the highlighted squares.

Ranks are rows across the board. Here the first rank is highlighted.

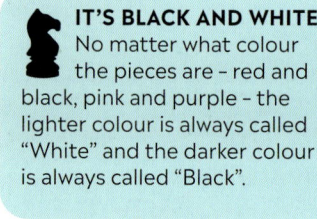

IT'S BLACK AND WHITE
No matter what colour the pieces are – red and black, pink and purple – the lighter colour is always called "White" and the darker colour is always called "Black".

One king
As the head of the army, the king is the tallest piece. Although the most important, he cannot move far and is therefore not powerful. If he cannot avoid capture, he is "checkmated" and the game is over.

One queen
The queen is your most powerful piece. She can attack almost half of the squares on the board from one position. She is both fast and wide-ranging.

Two bishops
Your bishops are recognized by the distinctive "cuts" in their heads – representing bishops' hats. Bishops are agile pieces that move swiftly along the diagonals.

Two knights
These unique pieces are the only ones that can leap over obstacles, and the only ones that don't travel in a straight line. In the often crowded conditions of the chess board, you will find your knights invaluable.

The king, queen, bishops, knights, and rooks are arranged on the back rows.

Rooks are placed in each corner.

The pawns, eight for each army, stand in front of the main fighting pieces.

Black's army is correctly set up.

Setting up the board

Firstly you must place the board between you and your opponent, who sits opposite you. A white corner square of the board must always be to the right of each player. Then you place the pieces in their correct positions. The white army and the black army are set up at opposite ends of the board, facing each other. The king and queen are in the middle. Then come the bishops, knights, and rooks spanning out on either side. Finally the pawns are placed on the row in front.

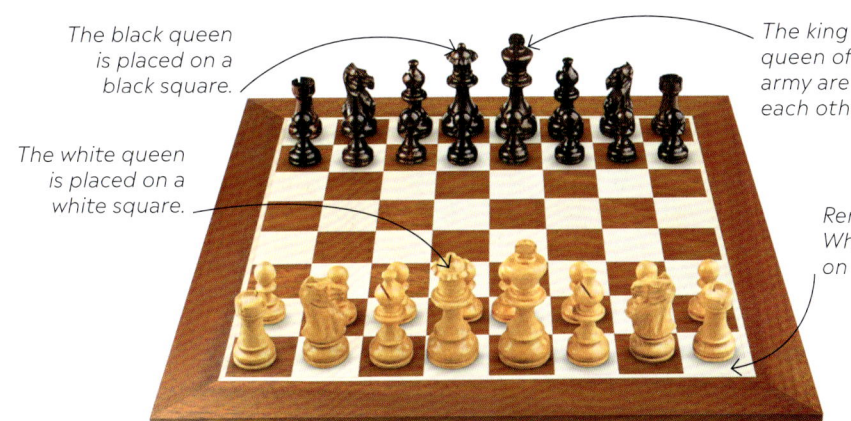

The black queen is placed on a black square.

The white queen is placed on a white square.

The king and queen of each army are opposite each other.

Remember! White square on the right.

Two rooks

This pair of sturdy pieces that use the ranks and files look like castles and in fact are frequently called "castles". Your rooks are the second most powerful pieces, after the queen, but they are also the hardest to get into the action.

Eight pawns

These are the footsoldiers of the chess board, and there are eight in each army. Your pawns often enter the action first. Pawns are the least powerful pieces – but they have ambition. If a pawn reaches the end of the board, it can be promoted, perhaps even to the status of the mighty queen.

The aim of the game

The aim of chess, simply, is to trap your opponent's king and deliver "checkmate". Actually doing it, however, isn't so simple. Chess is a battle of wits between two players, each controlling their own army. The battle can last for hours or end very suddenly. You can gain the advantage by steady pressure, building up your attack slowly by capturing enemy pieces, while keeping your own pieces safe. Or a well-aimed blow after only a few moves can end the game.

Battle it out!
Chess is one of the oldest war games in the world. The pieces represent the armies, and the board represents the battlefield. There is a white army and a black army. The two armies move towards each other and then the fight begins. Attacking and defending strategies are played out as though the players are real generals overseeing a real battle. The general with the best strategy and tactics will win the game.

Developing/capturing

Though checkmate is the aim of the game, you build up to it by weakening your enemy's army through capturing pieces. The idea is that your opponent will then be too weak to resist, and will not be able to defend the king. Players must first compete for a good position in the middle of the board. One player will get the upper hand, and will then be able to invade enemy territory, capture weak enemy pieces, or open up a decisive attack on the enemy king.

Checkmate
Checkmate comes as a result of the tactics and strategy of one player being superior to that of the other player's. The player who is "checkmated" (or "mated") has lost the game. Only more games can increase your skill and help you learn to be the victor in the next match.

White's general is pleased because they are playing an effective move.

Black's general will have to think of a way to improve their position.

White has captured three black pieces, taken them off the board, and put them aside.

Simple notation

How many languages do you know? English, probably, maybe some Mandarin or Hindi, or some other language. Perhaps you know the language of music, with its crotchets, quavers, and staves. Chess has its own language too, but it's much easier to learn. It's a simple way to name the squares and to describe the movement of pieces over the board.

The pieces

In chess diagrams, each piece is represented by a symbol. Although the symbols can be different colours, shapes, and sizes, it's usually easy to recognize them. In notation, each piece is given a letter. You always use capital letters when referring to the pieces.

This is the symbol for the king. In notation a king is written as just "K".

This is the symbol for the queen. In notation a queen is written as just "Q".

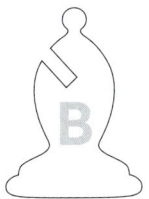

This is the bishop. In notation a bishop is written as just "B".

A knight is written as "N". The king took the "K" first!

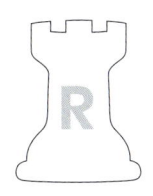

A rook is written as "R".

There are so many pawns that it is simpler to note them by their position on the board. The pawn has no letter.

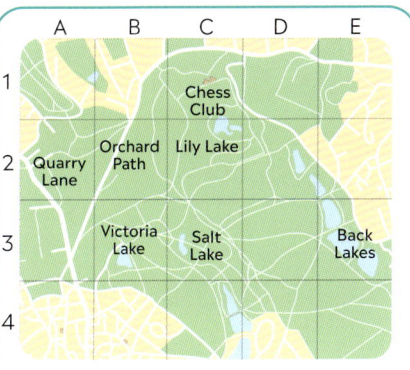

Check it out!

The chess board can be read in the same way as a map. Look at this map. The chess club is in square C1. If you can read a map, you can read a chess board.

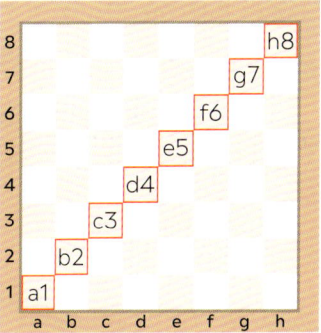

The board

The board is made up of 64 squares, in eight rows of eight squares. If we place the numbers 1 to 8 at the side of the board, and the letters a to h along the bottom of the board, by joining up the number and letter we can give every square its own name. The letter comes first, followed by the number. Have a look at the diagram to see how it works.

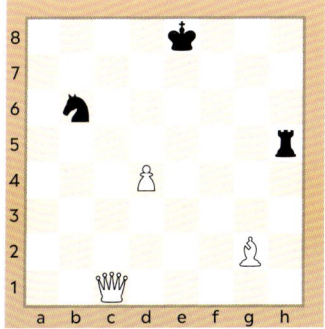

It's your move!

Look at the board. Can you write down where the black rook is? How about the black knight, black king, white queen, white pawn, and white bishop? For example, the white queen is on square c1.

Pawns

The pieces are ranked from the highest to the lowest, and nothing is lower than a pawn. In fact its name seems to come from the Old French *paon*, meaning "footsoldier". Yet the pawn is a fascinating piece, and many players see it as the soul of chess. What a pawn lacks in strength, it makes up for in numbers. The pawns take the brunt of early fighting, they control territory, and are the king's natural guardians.

Check it out!
In Lewis Carroll's *Alice through the Looking Glass*, many characters are inspired by chess pieces. Alice herself is a white pawn who eventually makes her way to the top of the board where she is promoted to a queen.

Advance!

A player often moves a pawn before anything else, just as a general might send in the footsoldiers before the cavalry on a battlefield. On its first move each pawn can move either one or two squares forwards. After that it can only move one square forwards at a time. Pawns can't move backwards.

The black general has decided to move this black pawn one square forwards in its first move.

The white pawn has moved two squares forwards, because it is its first move.

The pawns are lined up like footsoldiers at the start of a battle.

Capturing

Unlike all the other pieces, pawns do not capture in the same way that they move. They move straight forwards, but they capture diagonally forwards one square.

This pawn moves diagonally forwards to capture the knight.

This knight is removed from the board and the white pawn takes its place.

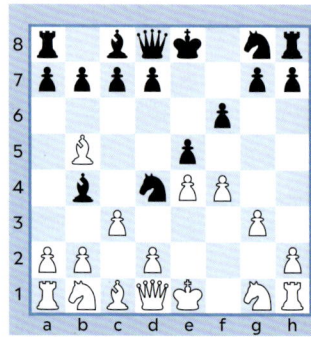

It's your move!
Look at this game position. Which black pieces can white pawns capture? (Answers on page 43.)

En passant

En passant means "in passing" in French. In chess it is a rule that prevents a pawn from slipping past an enemy pawn, by moving forwards two squares on its first move. *En passant* can happen anytime during a game. A pawn moving up two squares can be captured by an enemy pawn standing next to it. The enemy pawn, capturing diagonally, takes the position of the captured pawn as though it had only moved one square.

1 This white pawn, on its first move, moves two squares forwards.

2 It settles alongside an enemy pawn. The white pawn has moved past the square that the black pawn is diagonally attacking, which is marked in red.

3 Next move, the black pawn can capture the white pawn diagonally, as though the white pawn had only moved one square.

Promotion

Pawns have a special feature, which makes them individually precious, and often sways the result of a game. A pawn starts the game as the lowest piece, but if it reaches the opponent's end of the board – crossing six squares without mishap or capture – it can become a queen, a bishop, a knight, or a rook, depending on the piece that is most useful for the general at the time. Promotion refers to replacing the pawn with one of your pieces captured by the opponent. The queen is the most powerful piece on the board, so usually players would choose to promote their pawn to a queen. Pawn promotion is often called "queening".

A white pawn has reached the end of the board and become a queen.

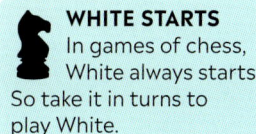

PROMOTING A PAWN TO A QUEEN
If you don't have an extra queen available, you can use an upside-down rook to represent a promoted queen.

The pawn game

Play this game with a friend, using only the pawns. This will give you a firm idea of how pawns move, capture, and promote. The *en passant* rule also applies, so watch out! The winner is the first to cross the board and promote a pawn. The game is a draw if both sides cannot move at all. Look at this example game.

WHITE STARTS
In games of chess, White always starts. So take it in turns to play White.

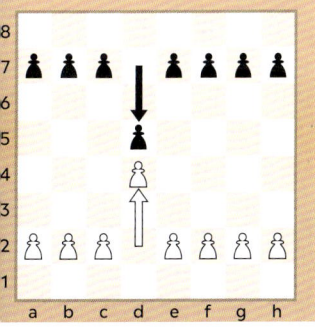

1 White has started and moved a pawn up two squares. Black has mirrored its move. Both pawns are now stuck.

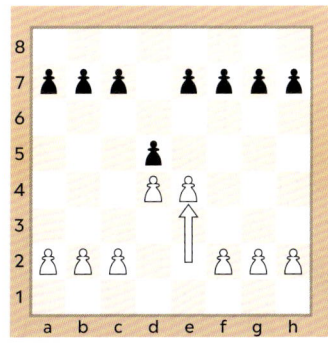

2 White has moved a second pawn up two squares. A mistake! It can be taken. Black makes the capture.

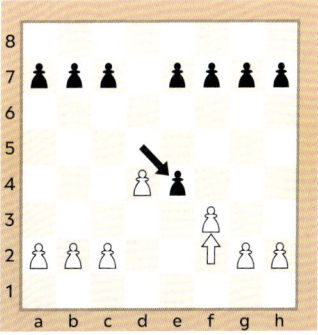

3 White moves a pawn up one square, and lays down a challenge to the advancing black pawn. Will Black capture again?

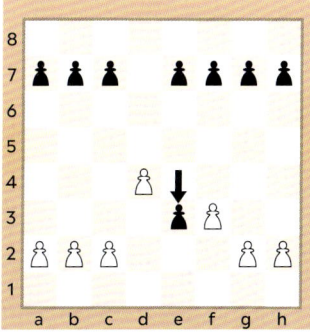

4 Black moves forwards. Good move! Now the black pawn cannot be stopped. Black will get a queen in two moves and win the game.

Bishops

Bishops once held powerful positions as the king's chief advisors, and the king would ask for their blessing before every battle. In chess, the bishops of each colour are a formidable pair. Like bishops of old, they are powerful pieces that often work together, one moving along the white diagonals and the other moving along the black diagonals. Between them they can cover all of the squares.

Moving

Bishops only move along the diagonals. They can move backwards and forwards and are especially effective if they are positioned in the middle of the board. Bishops are blocked if there is a piece in the way as they cannot jump. Notice how the bishop in the middle of the board controls 13 white squares (highlighted in blue), and the bishop on the edge controls only seven black squares (highlighted in green).

The "white-square" bishop is so-called because it only moves along the white diagonals (shown in blue).

The "black-square" bishop only moves along the black diagonals (shown in green).

Capturing

The bishops capture in the same way as they move: diagonally. The white-square bishop only captures pieces on the white squares, while the black-square bishop only captures on the black squares. Because of their wide range, bishops are useful in guarding long tracts of squares.

The white bishop moves along the white diagonal to capture the black knight.

The knight is removed from the board to sit out the rest of the game. The bishop takes its place.

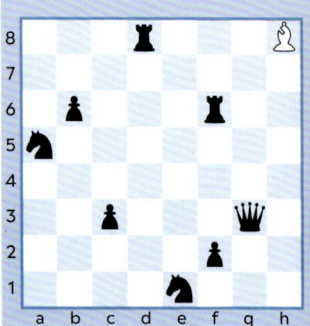

It's your move!
The white bishop can capture all the black pieces in eight moves. Black will kindly keep still for White's rampage. There are two ways of doing this. Can you work them out? (Answer on page 43.)

Knights

Most of the pieces on the board move in a straightforward way; the rook, queen, bishop, king, and even the pawn are variations on the straight or diagonal move. The knights, however, are governed by completely different rules. They travel in an L-shape and can also jump over obstacles, just like real horses.

Check it out!
Horses have been used in battle for centuries. In medieval times, their riders were brave soldiers, who were given the special title of "knight" by their king.

Moving

A knight can jump from one square to another, without touching the ground in between. This means it can jump over other pieces in an "L-shaped" move. The knight crosses two squares in a straight line, and then goes either one square to the right or one square to the left. Like bishops, knights have more power in the centre than on the edge. The knight in the centre can hit eight white squares (shown here in blue), while the knight on the edge can only hit three squares (shown in green).

The knight can hit a maximum of eight squares from one position.

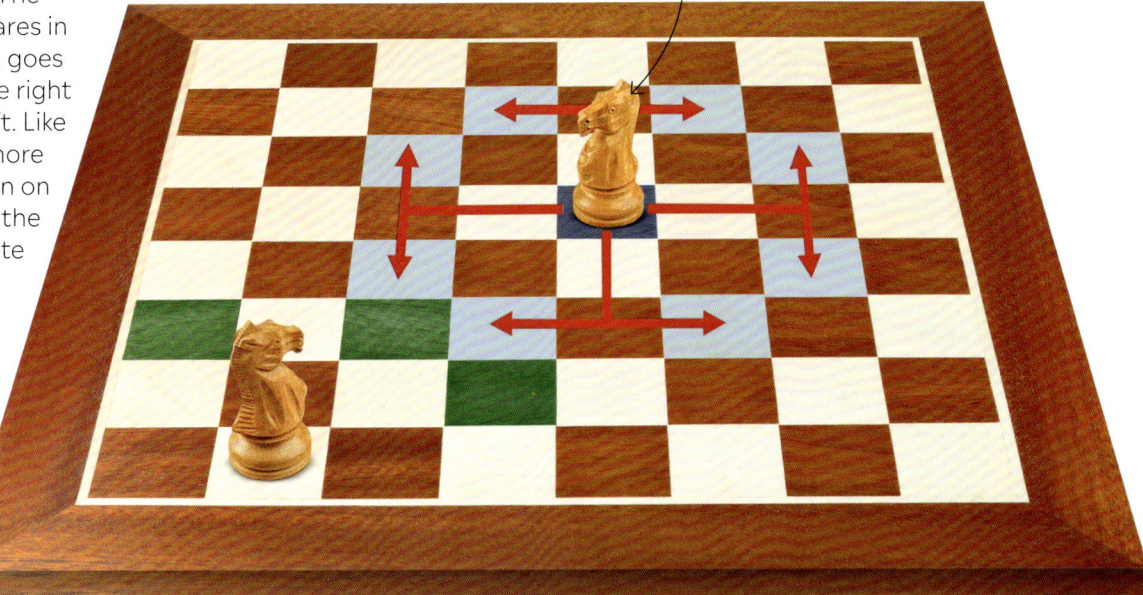

Capturing

The knight captures in the same way that it moves. It therefore has a maximum of eight squares that it can attack at any one time. Because it can jump, the knight never gets blocked in, and as a result can really "float like a butterfly and sting like a bee".

The white knight jumps in an L-shape onto the square occupied by the black pawn.

The pawn is removed from the board, and the knight takes its place.

It's your move!
The white knight can capture all the black pieces in six moves. Again, they will kindly stand still. Can you work out the two ways to do it? (Answer on page 43.)

Rooks

There are two rooks in each army. At the beginning of a game, they stand at the corners of the board, like fortresses guarding the outskirts. Rooks are often the last to enter the fray, but when they do, they make very efficient weapons of attack, second only to the queen.

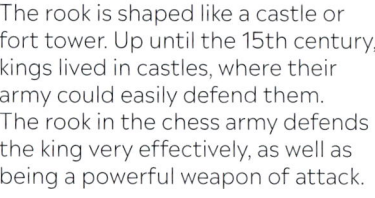

Castle defence
The rook is shaped like a castle or fort tower. Up until the 15th century, kings lived in castles, where their army could easily defend them. The rook in the chess army defends the king very effectively, as well as being a powerful weapon of attack.

Moving

The rook moves along the ranks and files of the chess board. It can access every square of the board, and at any one time it can control a maximum of 15 squares. A rook cannot jump over any other pieces, except when it makes a special move called "castling" (see page 22). Rooks rarely come into play at the beginning of a game, but once your rooks are brought into play, they can cover the board very well.

The rook is the only piece that has the same range on the edge and in the middle of the board – 14 squares.

Capturing

Like the other pieces, the rooks capture by occupying the place of an enemy piece. There must be empty squares between the rook and an enemy piece for it to capture as rooks can't jump. Because the rook can cover every square on the board, it is a dangerous attacking piece.

The bishop is now "dead wood" and is removed from the board.

The white rook moves along the rank to take the black bishop's place.

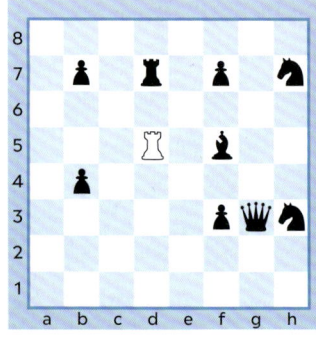

It's your move!
You have nine moves to capture all the black pieces with the white rook. All the white pieces are stuck and cannot move. Can you work out how to do it? (Answer on page 43.)

The queen

In the 15th century, the way the queen moved was changed forever. Originally she was one of the weakest pieces, advancing just one square at a time. Once she was given the power to move diagonally and horizontally over all the squares, the game came alive. While the queen stalks the board no piece is safe, and kings tremble behind their stockade of pawns.

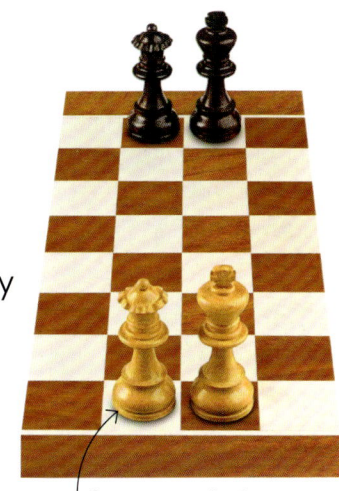

Queens are "colour conscious" at set up. They are placed on the square that matches their colour.

Moving

If you've absorbed the moves of the rook and bishop, you will have no trouble understanding the queen as she combines their moves. Your queen can hit a staggering 27 squares from one position, covering both the ranks and files, as well as the diagonals.

The queen moves in every direction. She can move as many squares as she wants, unless she is blocked by another piece. The queen cannot jump.

Capturing

The queen captures in the same way that she moves. She cannot jump over pieces in the way. Your queen is your most valuable piece and so you must be very careful that she isn't captured. If you lose her, you will find it hard to win against an enemy who still has a queen.

The white queen streaks across the board to capture the black knight.

The knight is removed from the board, and the queen takes its place.

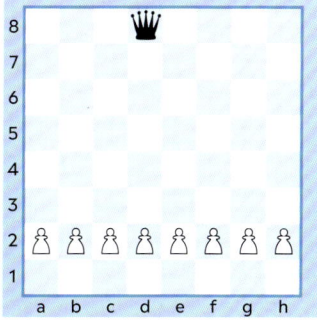

It's your move!
Play this game with a friend. The aim for White is to get one pawn to the other end of the board to be queened. The aim for Black is to prevent this from happening with just one rampaging queen.

The king

The most important piece is the king, although he is by no means the strongest. Unlike the other main pieces, your king can only shuffle along one square at a time. His safety is vital. If your opponent manages to trap your king, so that he cannot avoid capture, the game is over and you have lost. The downfall of the king, as in days of old, means the end for your whole army.

Check it out!

Ancient Persia's influence on the origins of chess is reflected in the language we use in the game. The word "checkmate", that tells us the king is trapped and the game over, comes from the Persian words *Shah mat*, meaning "the king is dead".

Moving

At any one time your king can move to the eight squares surrounding him, as long as he is not blocked by another piece, nor lands on a square that puts him in check (see page 21). He can move in any direction but only one square at a time. He is not speedy and cannot make hasty escapes. In a game, the king usually stays on the edge of the battlefield, behind a protective wall of pawns.

The king can move one square in any direction. The squares surrounding him can act as escape routes.

Capturing

The king captures in the same way that he moves. Don't forget that although he is weak, he can still capture, and this can sometimes get him out of sticky situations.

Here the white king moves diagonally one square to capture a black knight.

The knight is removed from the board and the king takes the knight's place.

Check

When the king is attacked by an enemy piece, it is called "check". If your king is in check, your next move has to be to get him out of check. You can do this by moving your king out of trouble, blocking the attack with another piece, or capturing the enemy piece that is threatening the king.

The white king is in check from the black bishop. He can escape by moving one square away from the bishop's attack, by capturing the bishop with his rook, or by blocking the attack with his bishop.

Checkmate challenge

Look at these diagrams. Can you find the move in each one that gives checkmate? You are playing as White, and it is your move. (Answers on page 43.)

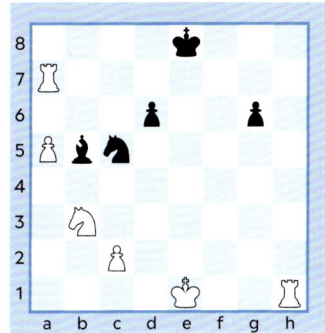

1 In this diagram, White can give checkmate in one move. The black king cannot move onto the rank covered by the rook on a7. What is the winning move?

Checkmate

"Checkmate" (or "mate" for short) is when one side's king is under attack and he cannot escape. No matter what move is made, the king can be captured and the game is lost. For this reason every move throughout the game is made with the ultimate aim of checkmate in mind. Checkmating your opponent can be achieved in just two moves, or it can be a long struggle that can take more than 50. Either way, giving checkmate is a thrill – you have won the battle.

Experienced players can see when a situation is hopeless and resign by knocking over their king before checkmate occurs.

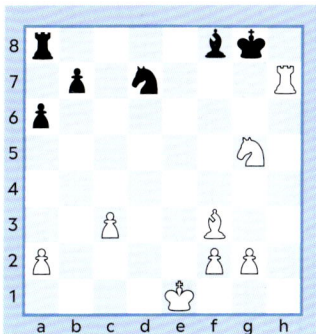

2 Here White can give checkmate by moving the bishop on f3. Which square should the bishop move to?

The black queen delivers the fatal blow.

The white king is in checkmate. There is nowhere for him to go and White has lost the game.

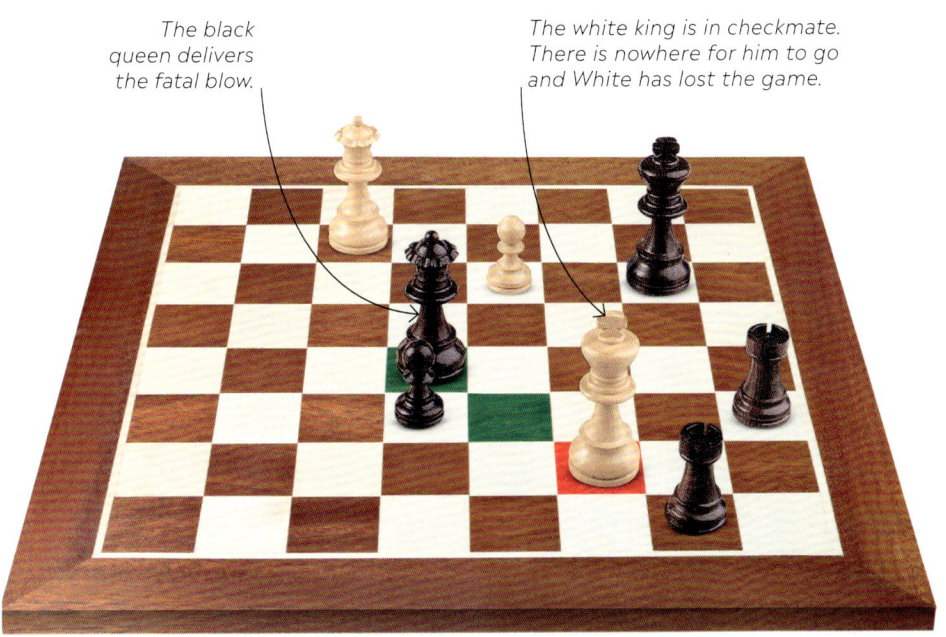

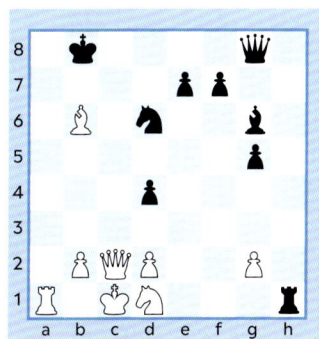

3 Here the black king is vulnerable and the white queen is ready to pounce. Where should she go?

King of the castle

It is important to understand the king's relationships with the other pieces. Here we look at "castling", a special rule that puts your king into safety, almost as though he is in a real castle. Once you have learnt the attacking strengths of your enemy's pieces, and how your pawns make effective guards, your king should be safe from ambush.

Check it out!
Castles were some of the only buildings safe enough for kings to live in. The "castling" move is an echo of the past and it is just as effective against attack as a real castle.

Castling

Both sides can tuck their kings into a corner, using a rule called "castling". Castling is the only time you can move two pieces at the same time – the king moves two squares, and the rook jumps over! Castling happens on the back row, behind the pawns. You can only castle if the squares are empty between the king and rook, and the king and rook have not yet moved.

There are spaces between the king and rook, so White is ready to castle. The king moves two squares right...

... and then the rook jumps over.

King's-side castling
This is when your king castles on his own side of the board. If both the knight and bishop have moved out of the way, so there are empty squares between the king and the rook, the king moves two squares towards the rook, and then the rook jumps over.

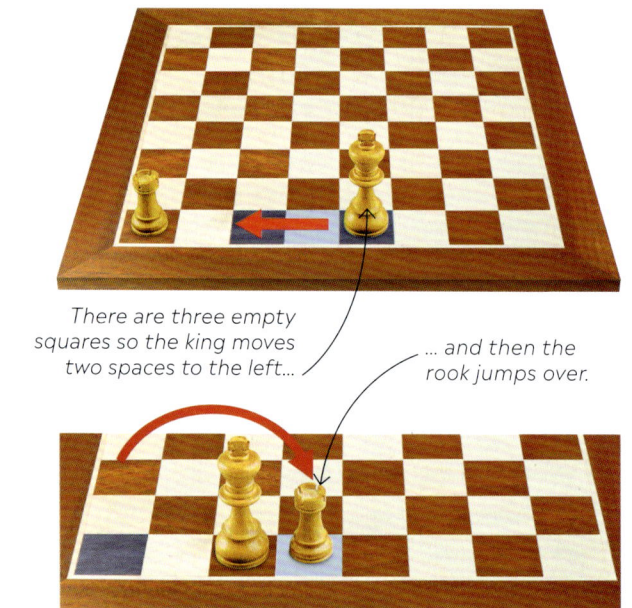

There are three empty squares so the king moves two spaces to the left...

... and then the rook jumps over.

Queen's-side castling
If the pieces on the queen's side of the board are moved out of the way – the queen, bishop, and knight – so that there are three empty squares between the king and the rook, you can also castle on this side. This is called queen's-side castling.

When you can't castle

There are three important situations when you can't castle: if the king passes through check on his way; if, by castling, you land in check; or when your king is already in check.

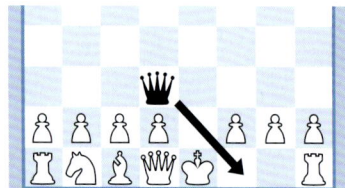

Through check
The coast seems clear for White to castle, but it is not. If White castles, the king will pass over a square attacked by Black's queen, and that's not allowed.

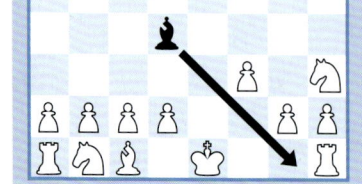

Into check
In this position, White is ready to castle. But the black bishop spoils the party. If White tries to castle, their king will land in check, and that's not allowed either.

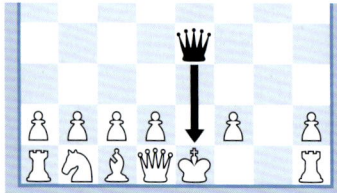

Out of check
The white king would dearly love to castle out of check. It would solve all his problems. Instead he must move, or block the attack with his queen.

Friend or foe?

The king's best friends are the pawns. Clustered around him at the beginning, they provide protection at all stages of the game. The king also has enemies; your opponent is planning to trap your king and will use every weapon at their disposal. The most powerful weapon is the queen. Look at this game, called "Fool's Mate".

1 White moves a pawn forwards two squares. Black moves a pawn forwards one square. Both players have made conventional opening moves.

2 White's second pawn moves up, forgetting how important it is to keep the king under guard – White has moved a pawn to disastrous effect!

3 Black's queen streaks in and delivers checkmate to the powerless white king. The white king has been deserted by his pawns and lost the game in just two moves.

Enemy strength

Try this simple test to measure the strength of enemy pieces. From this you will see why the queen is the most dangerous attacking piece.

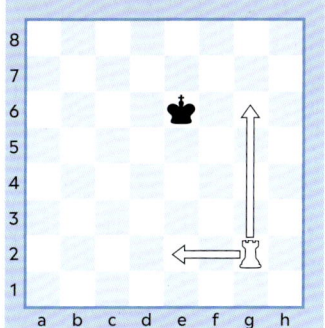

Rook's strength

Put a white rook and a black king on the chess board. You could move the rook to one of two squares, in this diagram g6 and e2, and from both positions the rook could call check.

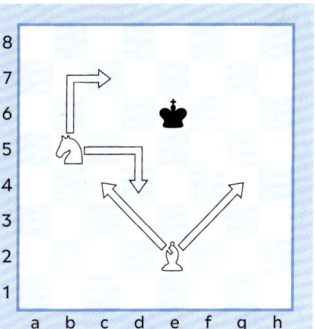

Bishop's and knight's strength

Now put a white knight and a white bishop onto the board. There is a maximum of two squares they can move to that give check for each piece.

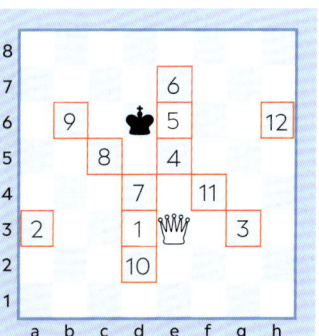

Queen's strength

Lastly put a white queen onto the board. From any one position the queen can move to give check from a multitude of squares. In this diagram there are 12 (although squares next to the king are dangerous for her unless she is supported).

Further notation

It's time to learn a few more of the signs and symbols that will help you to follow the moves in the rest of the book. After a bit of practice, you'll be able to use what you learn to amaze your friends and family by playing chess without a board or pieces!

Moving and capturing

We show how the pieces move by naming the square that they move to.

  Rc2 means "rook moves to square c2"
  e3 means "pawn moves to e3"

You can tell which piece is moving because it is the only one that can move to the named square. The rare cases you can't tell are called "ambiguous moves" (see right). The letter of the piece (always a capital letter) comes before the square it moves to. In the case of the pawn, because it has no letter, you just name the square that it moves to.

Captures are shown by placing an "x" in the middle of a formula: *Qxb8* means "queen captures at b8". For pawn captures, you name the file that the pawn came from: *exf4* means "pawn on the e-file captures at f4".

This pawn move is written in notation as "a5".

This rook move is written as "Rd7".

This white queen moving to capture the black bishop is written as "Qxc2".

This white pawn moving to capture the black knight is written as "gxf3".

Ambiguous moves

Sometimes two of the same pieces of the same colour can go to the same square. This usually happens with rooks and knights. To identify which piece moves, you specify where the moving piece came from, i.e. which rank or file, as well as naming the square it moves to. Here, the knights at d7 and g8 can both move to f6. The rooks can both move to a4.

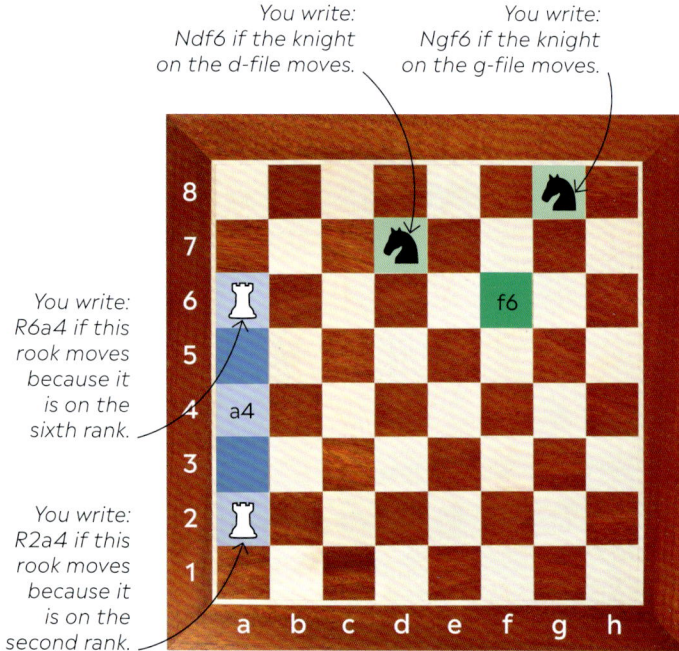

You write: Ndf6 if the knight on the d-file moves.

You write: Ngf6 if the knight on the g-file moves.

You write: R6a4 if this rook moves because it is on the sixth rank.

You write: R2a4 if this rook moves because it is on the second rank.

Notation checklist

Castling: O-O means castles on the king's side
             O-O-O means castles on the queen's side

Check: + at the end of a move e.g., Bb5+ means "bishop moves to b5 and gives check"

Checkmate: # at the end of a move e.g., Qh5# is "queen moves to h5 and gives checkmate"

Promotion: e.g., e8=Q means a pawn moves to e8 and is promoted to a queen; f8=N means a pawn moves to f8 and becomes a knight

Following a game

Practise your notation skills by following this game on your chess board. Set up your board in the start position. Read the notation and make the moves, three moves at a time. Notice the way the games are written with each move numbered, and separate columns for White's moves and Black's moves. This game is a famous game, called "Boden's mate", played in London in 1853.

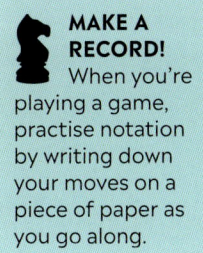

MAKE A RECORD!
When you're playing a game, practise notation by writing down your moves on a piece of paper as you go along.

1.	e4	e5
2.	Nf3	d6
3.	c3	f5

↑ *White's moves* ↑ *Black's moves*

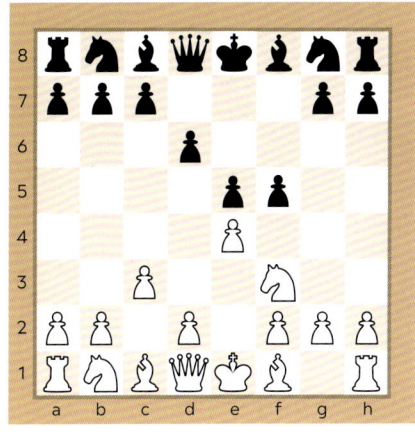

1 Remember that pawns have no letter, so they are indicated by the position they move to. Also that "N" means one of the knights.

4.	Bc4	Nf6
5.	d4	fxe4
6.	dxe5	exf3

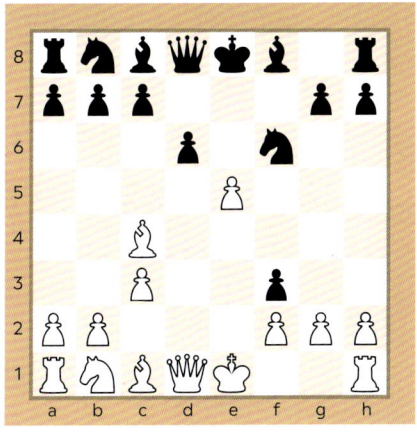

2 Now one of White's bishops has moved into the game. And there have been some neat pawn captures. Both players are jockeying for position.

7.	exf6	Qxf6
8.	gxf3	Nc6
9.	f4	Bd7

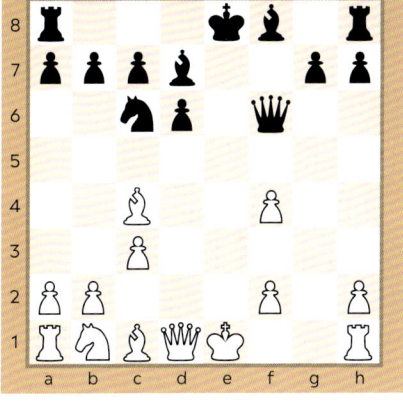

3 Black's powerful queen has entered the fray and has already made her presence felt.

10.	Be3	0-0-0
11.	Nd2	Re8
12.	Qf3	Bf5

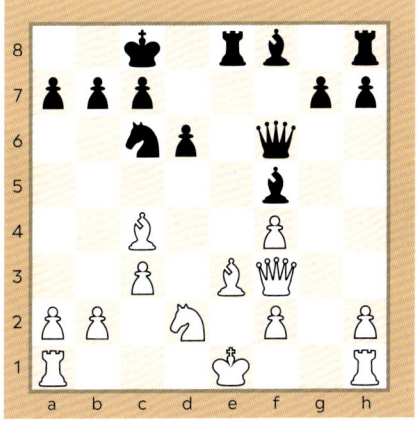

4 Following so far? Good. See how neatly the black king was tucked away when Black castled on the queen's side. White is looking a little vulnerable.

13.	0-0-0	d5
14.	Bxd5	Qxc3+
15.	bxc3	Ba3#

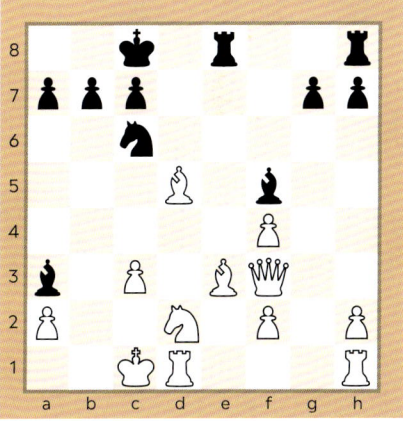

5 Black seemed foolish to lose the queen. But Black had a good plan... White is undone by Black's bishops. Checkmate!

It's your move!

Have a go at these two exercises, and find out if you're a natural code-breaker. (Answers on page 43.)

1 Look at the four moves made by White in this diagram and write them down in chess notation on a piece of paper.

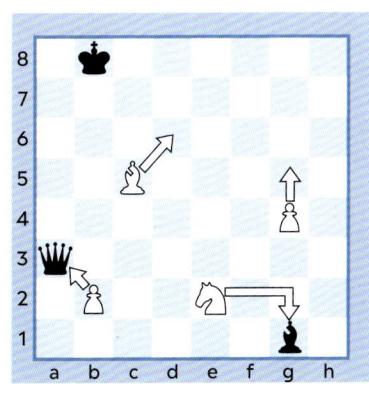

2 Crack the codes for this short game and do the moves on your chess set. You should end up with the checkmate position shown here. This is called "Scholar's mate".

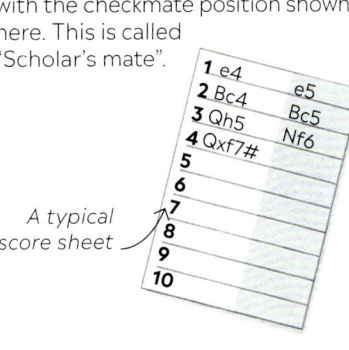

1	e4	e5
2	Bc4	Bc5
3	Qh5	Nf6
4	Qxf7#	
5		
6		
7		
8		
9		
10		

A typical score sheet

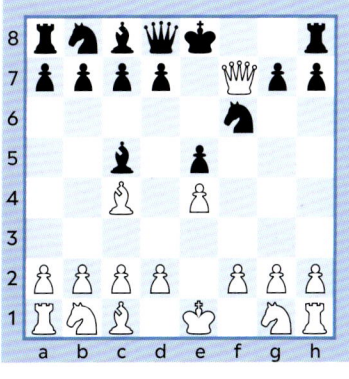

Opening

If you have followed everything so far, you are equipped with enough knowledge to play a game. You can move your pieces around the board, capture enemy pieces, and maybe even get checkmate. However, to play well you will need to understand the second half of this book, starting with the first phase of a chess game – called the "opening". There are more books written on the opening than on any other part of the game, and more than nine million possible positions after only three moves. Do you have to learn all these positions by heart? No. With just a few ideas you can play the opening very well.

Starting your game sets the scene for the battle ahead. If you play a good opening, you will have a good basis for attack later in the game.

Light brigade

In the first stage of the opening, only the pawns, bishops, and knights should be brought into play. This "light brigade" is used for initial skirmishes and for gaining a good central position. The more valuable queen and rooks make up the "heavy brigade" (see pages 28-29).

Five opening rules

If you decide your opening moves based on the following five rules, you will get off to an excellent start. These rules are relevant to all chess players, whether you are a beginner or a Grandmaster (player with international tournament victories). They are simple and easy to follow. Keep in mind that opening play is about gaining a strong position on the board from which to launch your attack, not for embarking on an immediate onslaught.

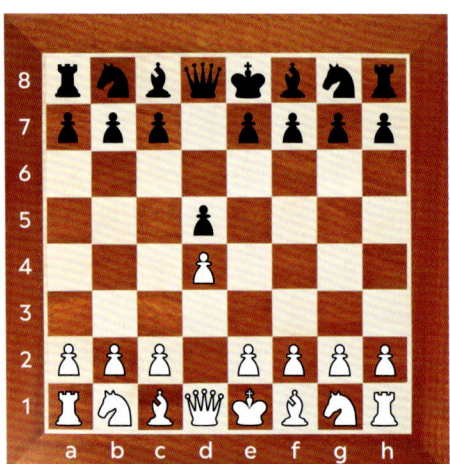

1 Pawns in the centre
Place one or two pawns in the centre. The centre of the board is where the first power struggle takes place, and whoever controls more of the midfield controls the game. Once the pawns have taken up position in the midfield, it's quite hard to dislodge them, so they may stay there for a long time.

2 Knights and bishops in the centre
This is an important rule. Send your knights and bishops into the centre. This will mean moving pawns to clear the path of your bishops, which can't jump. Knights, bishops, and pawns are your "light brigade" and need to be moved before your queen and rooks – the "heavy brigade".

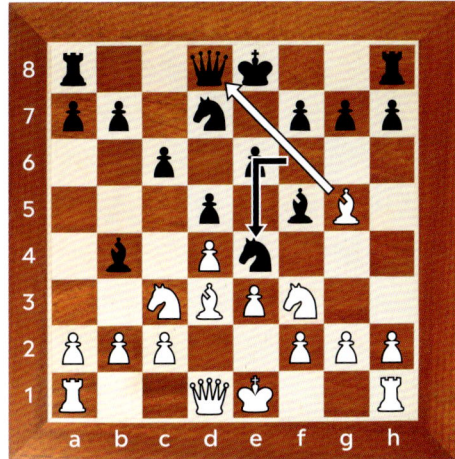

3 Move each piece once

As we have seen, the opening is about putting your pieces into good positions near the centre, ready for action. Your attacks come later. If you move the same piece around, making attacks, you'll soon end up with one piece fighting an entire army. Move each piece once instead.

4 Guard and capture

Be careful with the placing of your pieces. If your opponent can capture, make sure you can recapture so the armies stay level. Here Black has made a mistake. Moving the knight to e4 means that White can capture the queen!

5 Castle your king

Make your king safe by castling early. Castling removes your king from the centre and puts him on the edge, behind a stockade of pawns. In this picture below, the game has continued as though Black hasn't lost the queen. When you are playing, you should aim for an opening position like this.

LOOK AND LEARN
If you take opportunities to watch or study real chess games, you will find it easier to become a good player yourself.

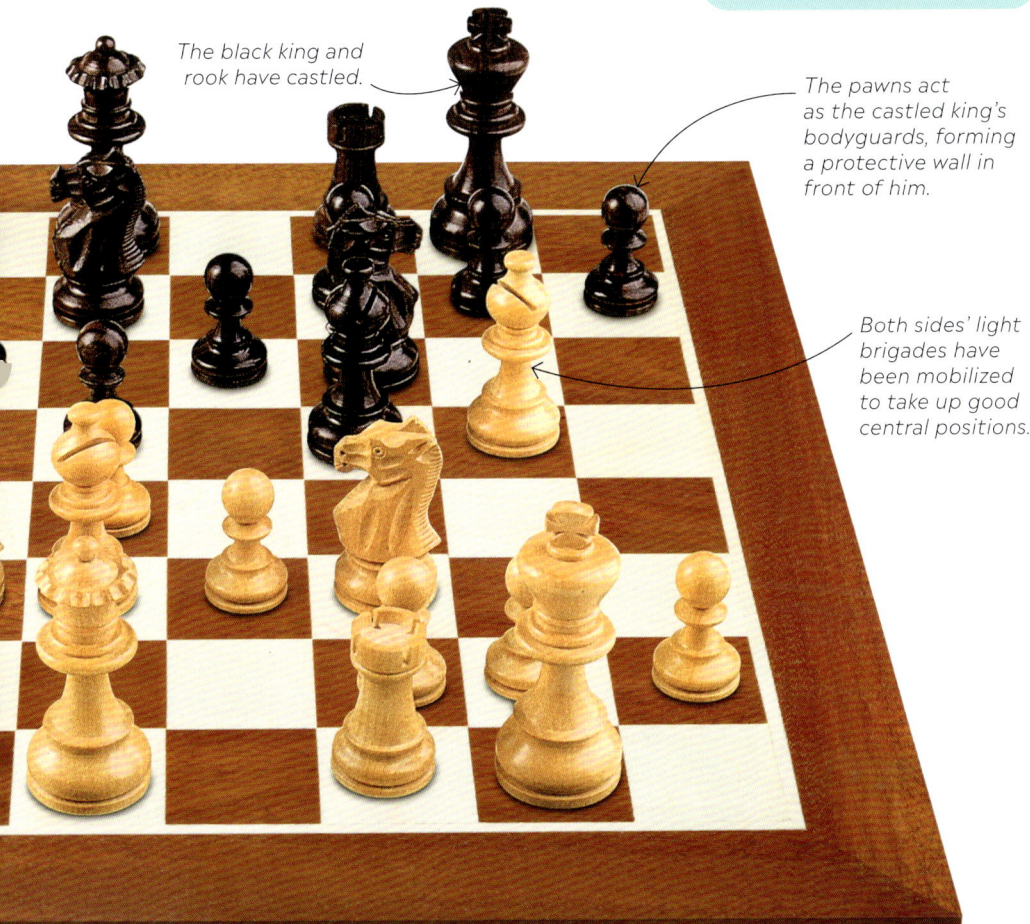

The black king and rook have castled.

The pawns act as the castled king's bodyguards, forming a protective wall in front of him.

Both sides' light brigades have been mobilized to take up good central positions.

It's your move!
Before you play your first game of chess using the new opening rules, test yourself on these positions. Choose the best move out of the three options. In all these positions you are playing White. (Answers on page 43.)

1 Choose a move!
a. Pawn to e4
b. Pawn to h4
c. Knight to h3

2 Choose a move!
a. Bishop to b5
b. Knight to a3
c. Pawn to d3

3 Choose a move!
a. Knight to f3
b. Pawn to e5
c. Knight to c3

The major pieces

By following the five rules of the opening, you are already getting off to a good start. But so far we have not looked at bringing the major pieces into play – your queen and rooks. They make up the "heavy brigade" and are extremely powerful and valuable pieces – rather like owning two tanks and a rocket launcher. With these weapons you can do immense damage to the enemy position. However, you do need to be careful with them. You need a plan of action that will put them into strong positions without exposing them to danger.

The heavy brigade

Unlike the "light brigade" (the pawns, knights, and bishops) the "heavy brigade" (queens and rooks) should not be placed in the centre straightaway. You must deploy them further back, and always keep in mind "minimum exposure, maximum power".

The queens in both armies move off the back rows to well-covered squares.

The rooks are free to move to open or half-open files.

Minimum exposure

Your major pieces are important to your eventual victory, so you must be very careful with them. The queen and rooks should fire at the enemy from a distance at the rear of the field, where enemy units cannot easily attack them. It's a good idea to move your queen off the back rank, bringing her into play and freeing up the back row for the rooks to move along. Pawns need to be cleared out of the way to get the rooks into the action. An "open" file has no pawns on it. A "half-open" file has pawns of one colour on it.

Maximum power

Clearing the way for your rooks is your priority at this stage (maximum power). Castling is a good way to get your rooks out of the corner, as well as to protect your king. Then, if you can move your rooks to an open or half-open file, so much the better. Your idea should be to have both the rooks and the queen in strong positions but not too far forward.

The white rook moves across to a half-open file.

This file is open. White's other rook can move here next move.

An opening

Now we shall follow the course of an opening, and show how the rooks and the queen are brought into play, keeping in mind "minimum exposure, maximum power". Make all the moves on your chess board.

1.	e4	c5
2.	Nf3	d6
3.	Bb5+	Bd7
4.	Bxd7+	Nxd7
5.	0-0	Ngf6

6.	Nc3	g6
7.	d4	

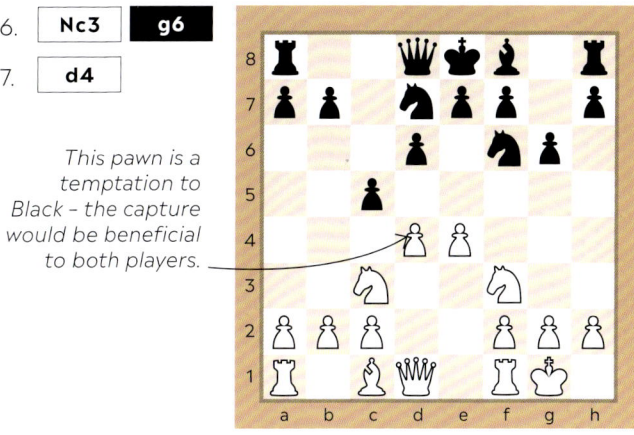

This pawn is a temptation to Black – the capture would be beneficial to both players.

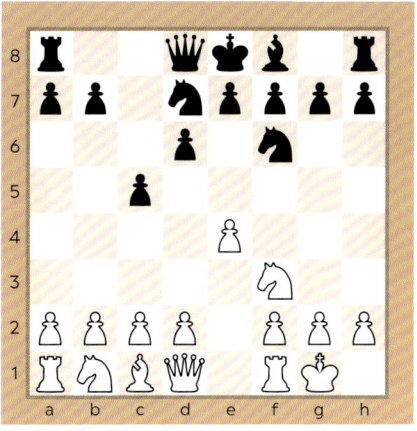

1 Five moves have been made. The two sides have exchanged bishops and advanced their light brigades. A good central position is the aim for both players.

2 White is now offering an exchange to Black. Black can capture White's pawn at d4 and White can recapture with the knight on f3. It would be to both players' advantage to create open files for later deployment of their rooks.

7.	...	cxd4

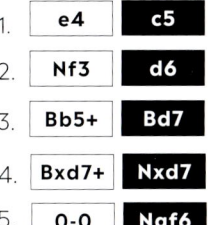

INTERRUPTED NOTATION
"..." shows that White has already moved. For example, in step 2, White's seventh move was d4 (see above). Black's following seventh move is preceded by "..." to show that White has already moved.

8.	Nxd4	Bg7
9.	Be3	0-0

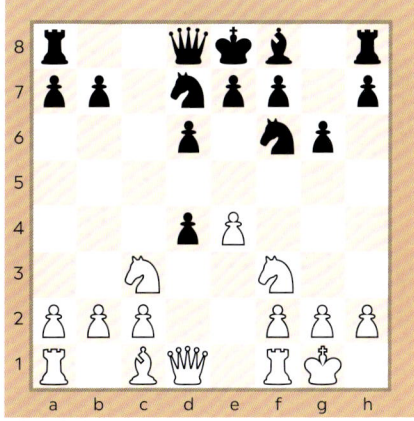

3 Black has acted as expected and has captured White's pawn. White will of course immediately recapture with the knight on f3. Black's c-file and White's d-file are now half-open.

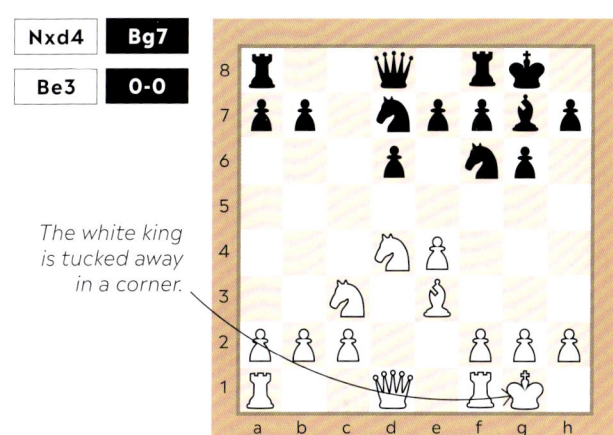

The white king is tucked away in a corner.

4 Next, both players move their bishops off the back rows, following the five rules of the opening as well as clearing space for the rooks behind them. White remembers the important opening rule of castling early.

10.	Qe2	Rc8
11.	Rad1	

The light brigades are in good central positions.

The heavy brigades have been deployed well by both sides.

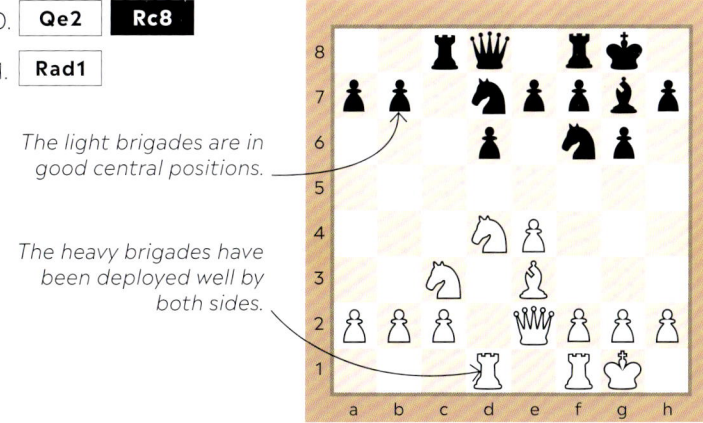

5 White moves the queen off the back row, and both Black and White move their rooks onto half-open files.

11.	...	a6
12.	f4	Qc7

The black queen cannot be easily attacked this far back.

6 The black queen is also moved off the back row to a safe position at the rear. Both generals have directed their armies well and kept to the rules of the opening. It's still anyone's game.

Key techniques

We can dream of being a pop star, a famous actor, or a footballing hero, but behind any success there are months of preparation, practice, and setbacks. To be a champion chess player takes the same kind of dedication, and the foundations of your success will be your ability to learn basic attacking and defending techniques. We are now moving into the important "middlegame" phase of a chess game, and start by introducing piece value.

Value

There is a value system that you can use to guide you. Your pawns are worth one point each, your knights and bishops are worth three points each, your rooks are worth five points, and your queen is worth nine points. Your king, of course, is priceless.

| 1 | 3 | 3 | 5 | 9 |

Capturing and value

Capturing is a very precise skill. At every move you should be working out all the possible captures you can make and rank them in order of their points value. The best captures are the ones that win the most points. On this board (below) White can make two captures: Nxc8 and Qxd6. Nxc8 is the best capture because the black queen is worth nine points. Capturing the bishop would only gain White three points. Capturing your opponent's strong pieces, while holding on to your own, is a sure way to eventual victory.

Recapture

In a game of chess, many pieces that you may want to attack are defended. You can capture an enemy piece, only to find that you are then captured back. This is called "recapture". In a game you must decide who gains or loses after a capture and recapture. You do this by measuring how many points, according to the value system, have been "exchanged". So if your bishop takes a pawn and is then recaptured, you have got the worst of the bargain. You deduct one point for the pawn from the three points for the bishop and find that your opponent has won two points. It's simple maths!

Taking the black queen is an excellent capture for White, worth nine points!

Capturing the black bishop will give White a reasonable three points, but capturing the queen is much better.

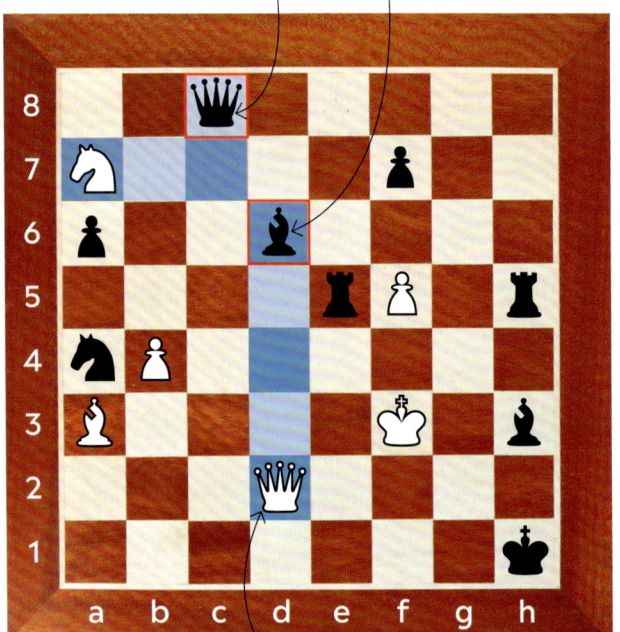

White's queen can capture Black's bishop, but always study the board to see if there are any better captures you can make.

Here the white bishop captures the black rook and is recaptured by Black's queen. White has gained two points, as a rook is worth two points more than a bishop.

Safe move

Moving your pieces around the chess board is like walking through a minefield. However, there is one big difference. None of the mines on the chess board are hidden. You can scan the board and see just which squares are under attack. Therefore, before you make a move, make sure you have checked that the square you are about to land on is safe. In this picture (below) there are only a few squares that White can move to that are entirely safe.

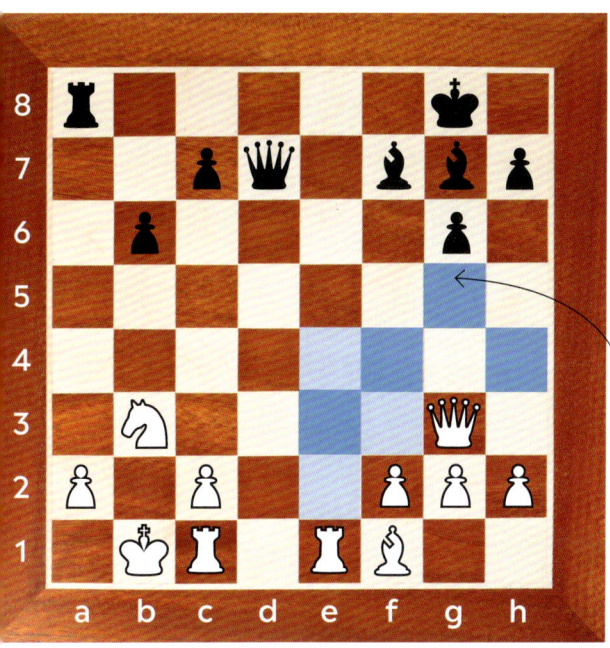

The blue squares are completely safe for White to move to. The other squares on the board can all be attacked by Black.

Mental checklist

Before you move, run through these questions in your head.
1. What is your best move/best capture?
2. By moving a piece, are you leaving any other piece undefended?
3. Are any of your pieces about to be captured?
4. If so, what can you do to defend yourself?

Safe-enough move

The further you advance into enemy territory, the more you find the squares are guarded by enemy pieces. However, you can still advance your pieces into good positions, provided they are adequately defended by their comrades. Therefore an important technique to master is the safe-enough move. This is where you move to a square attacked by an enemy piece, but you can recapture on that square and do not lose points overall as a result.

Nc5 is a safe-enough move. The knight could be captured by the black rook on c8, but Black dare not capture as they would lose points when White then recaptures with the pawn on b4.

Qh6 is also a safe-enough move. True, Black could play Qxh6, but White could then recapture, Bxh6, and the points would be level.

It's your move!

Look at each of these diagrams and work out the moves. (Answers on page 43.)

1 How many captures can White make? Write each one down and rank them according to how many points you could gain from each capture. Which is the best capture?

2 What captures can White make? There are four possibilities. Which is the best capture assuming that Black will recapture if they can?

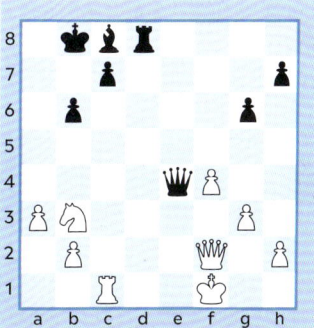

3 Write down the ten moves that are entirely safe for White (moving to squares that the enemy does not attack at all). Well done if you find all ten!

4 White can make the following moves: Rd4, Bxc7, Rd7, and Be5. Which moves are safe, not safe, or safe enough?

Attack and defend

Making precise, accurate attacks on enemy pieces is part of your technique. However, half of the moves in a chess game are made by your opponent, so knowing how to defend your pieces is also important. Chess is like a dance, except the idea is to tread on your opponent's toes as often as possible, while keeping your own feet out of danger.

Keeping time

In tournaments players are given 2-3 minutes on average to play each move. They are timed by a special clock with two faces. After making a move, a player hits the nearest button on top of the clock. The other clock then starts timing the other player.

Making threats

A simple threat is an attack on an undefended enemy piece or a piece of higher value. Threats force your opponent to waste moves in avoiding attack and help you to establish a strong position. If your threats result in captures, you will gain strength, but any threats you make must be safe or safe-enough moves.

An effective threat

On this board (right), White moves a bishop up to threaten the black knight at d6. This is a safe-enough move, because although the bishop can be captured by Black's queen, White could recapture with the knight on d3 and Black would lose the queen. Black must think of some other way to avoid the danger.

Bb4 is a safe-enough move, which makes an effective threat against Black's knight at d6.

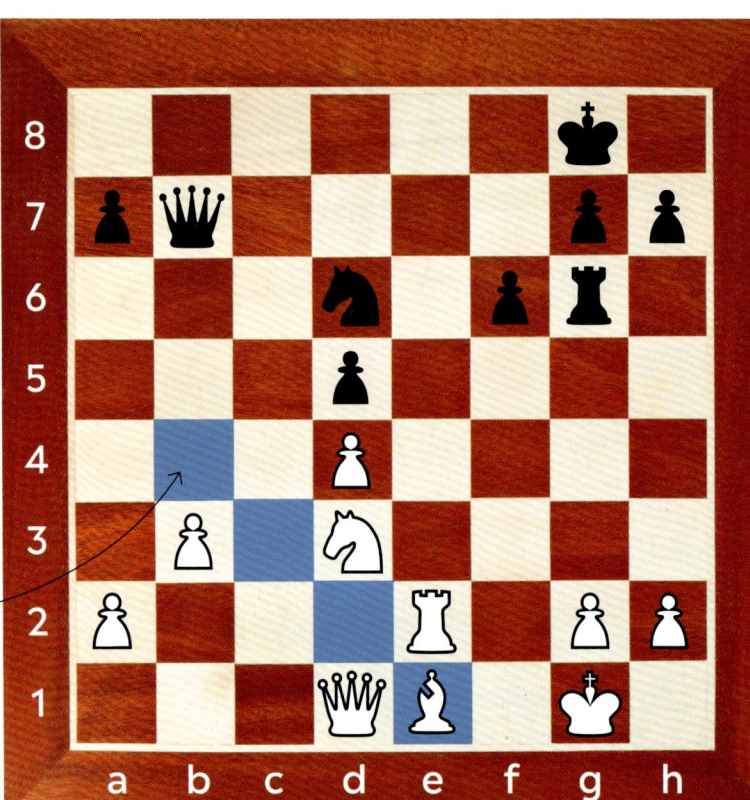

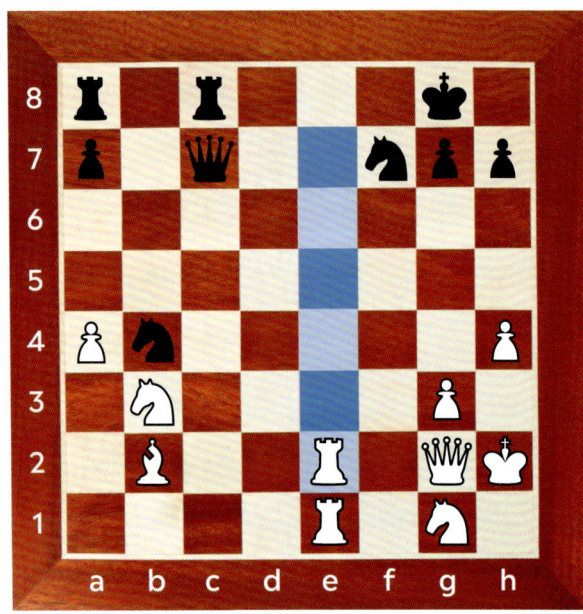

Rooks working in pairs

The rook-to-e7 move makes a threat – against Black's queen at c7. True, the queen can capture White's rook, but White is quite happy with that deal because the rook is guarded by White's other rook on e1. This is a very effective way to use your rooks.

It's your move!

Improve your attacking skills by making threats on enemy pieces. You are White and it's White's move. (Answers on page 43.)

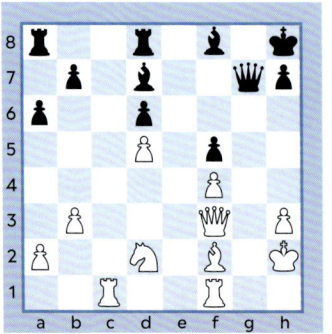

1 Mobilize your troops to make an attack! Remember that all threats must be safe or safe-enough moves.

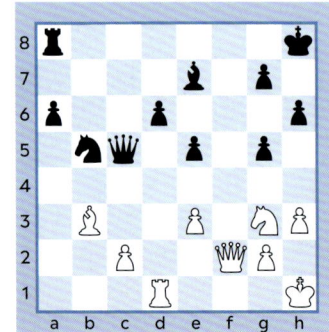

2 There are seven possible threats in this position. Can you find them all?

Defending against threats

While you are making good moves, and making threats, your opponent will be doing the same. To avoid enemy threats, there are five main methods of defence. Look at the positioning on the five chess diagrams. Black's rook at f7 is attacking the white rook at f3. Each diagram shows a different defensive technique.

Defensive moves
1. Move away.............................Run!
2. Capture the enemy...........Fight back!
3. Support your piece..........Get other pieces to help!
4. Block the attack..................Use a shield!
5. Counter-attack....................Cause a diversion!

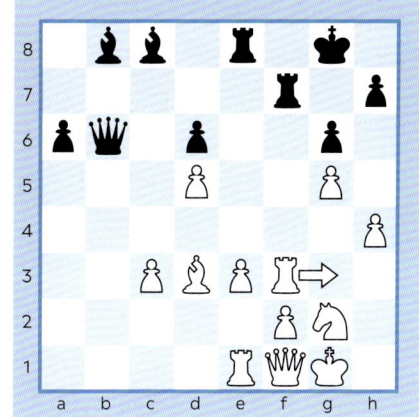

1 Move away
In this diagram, White can reduce the threat from Black's rook at f7 by moving the threatened rook to g3.

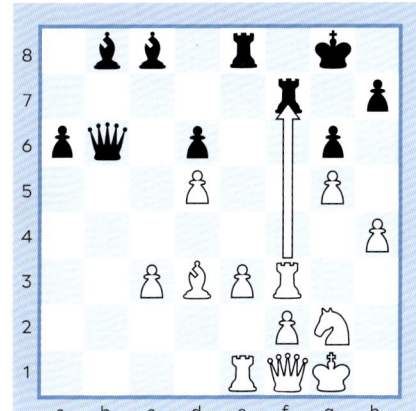

2 Capture the enemy
White's rook can, of course, capture the black rook – it will be recaptured, but it's an equal exchange.

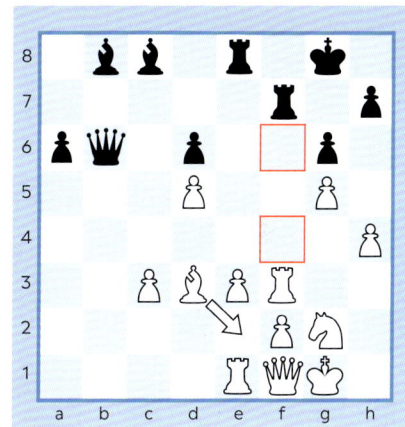

3 Support your piece
White can defend the rook by moving a bishop to e2 or moving the rook to f4 or f6 (which are guarded by pawns). If the black rook carries out its threat, White can recapture.

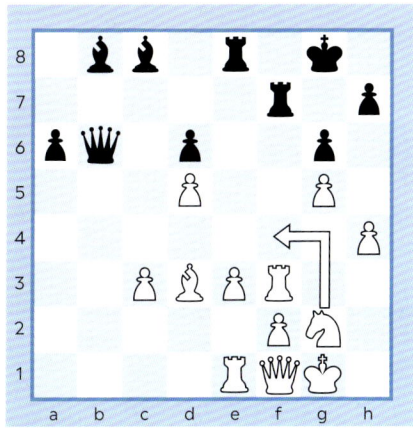

4 Block the attack
Here White chooses to move a knight in front of the threatened rook to block the attack from Black's rook.

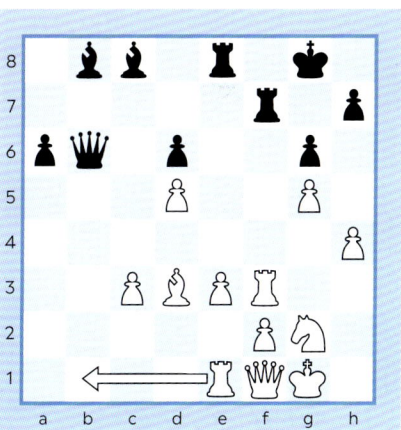

5 Counter-attack
Here White's other rook moves to threaten Black's queen. This tactic means that White doesn't waste a move, and it throws a spanner in the works. A counter-attack only works well if you attack a piece of equal or greater worth.

It's your move!
Look at the diagrams and work out all the possible defensive moves that White can make. (Answers on page 43.)

1 Black's queen is threatening White's knight at h3. What defensive moves can White make against the attack?

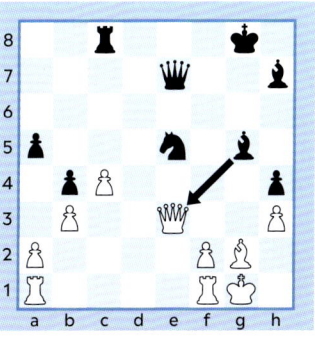

2 Black's bishop is threatening White's queen at e3. What moves can White make to avoid losing the queen?

Tactics

The foundation of your success will be the techniques you have already learnt. However, you can often speed up the winning process if you gain a knowledge of tactics. Between strong and equally matched players, tactical ability will turn the game one way or another. The main tactical ideas are the fork, the pin, and the discovered attack.

Knight forks

The greatest fork moves of all are made by your knight, which can threaten eight pieces at the same time. In this diagram, the knight can move to c7 and put three pieces under attack.

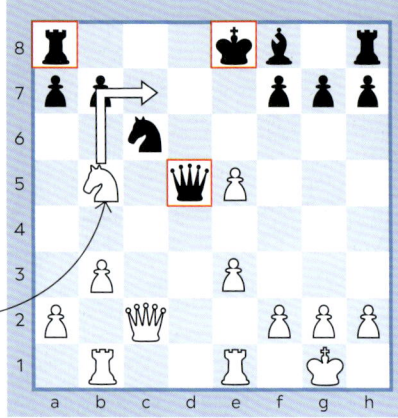

This knight, by moving to c7, makes a devastating fork, attacking the black king at e8, the rook at a8, and the queen at d5.

The fork

The fork is a tactical move where one piece attacks two or more pieces at the same time. This effective tactic makes it very difficult for your opponent to escape with all pieces unscathed, and usually results in a capture. Every single piece on the chess board can fork – even the humble pawn.

The white pawn forks both black rooks. Though one rook can escape in the next move, the other will be captured.

Discovered attack

After torturing your opponent with forks and pins (see page 35), you can also drop in a few discovered attacks. On the chess board nothing is hidden – all the pieces and all the squares are in full view. The only thing you cannot know is the future and the thoughts in your opponent's head. The discovered attack is the nearest thing you can get to concealment since you do one thing, but threaten another. Look at this example.

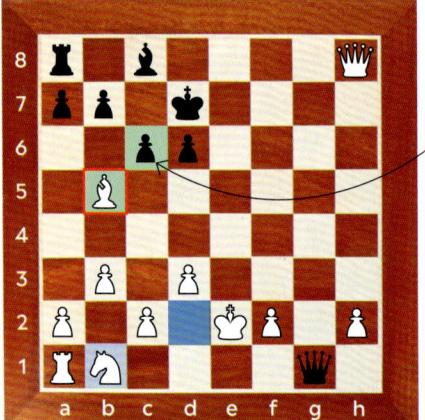

Black's pawn captures White's bishop.

1 Both sides have been going hammer and tongs at each other, and now, during a lull in the action, White decides to bring out a knight to d2. Thinking little of it, Black continues with their plan to capture the white bishop at b5 with a pawn.

White's rook moves to capture Black's queen.

2 Now the true point of White's plan is revealed – the white rook at a1 captures Black's queen! White's tactical play has paid off and put their army at a massive advantage.

The pin

A pin is another effective tactic. It is an attack on a piece which, if it tries to move, leaves a more valuable piece open to capture. This can sometimes gain you an advantage or even lead to complete paralysis of an enemy piece. With this tactical weapon you can really weaken your opponent.

This black bishop is pinning the white knight to the king.

The knight cannot move or the king will be in check.

A pawn is guarding the knight.

A pinned pawn

Here the pinned black pawn at d5 can't be guarded, can't move, and White will capture it in their next move with the bishop at b3. Not only will Black lose a pawn, but Black's king will also be in check.

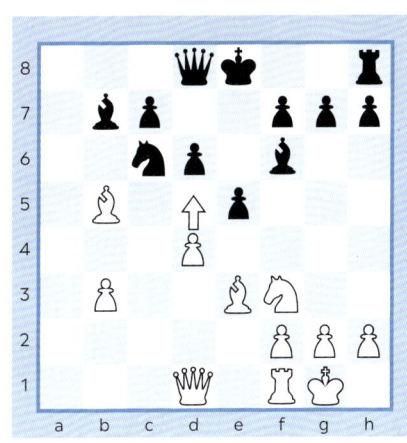

Under pressure

White's bishop at b5 is pinning the black knight at c6, who is protecting the king and is securely defended by the bishop at b7. But White attacks the knight again with a pawn, moving from d4 to d5. Now Black stands to lose a knight.

A killer blow

A discovered attack can be even more deadly if you can get the piece that moves to do some attacking work. Look at this situation. Black's pawn moves forwards and Black delivers check with a discovered attack from the bishop. White has to escape check and cannot react to the threat posed to the queen by the black pawn. Next move White will lose the queen.

Next, the black pawn will capture White's queen.

First, White will have to move their king to get it out of check.

Endgame

We have seen how games can end after only a few moves with a neat checkmate. But many games do not finish like that. In fact, though your opponent may be several pieces behind, it is certainly possible to avoid checkmate for a very long time. The term used to describe the end of chess games, when there are only a few pieces left, is "endgame". There are particular skills that you need to play effectively in endgame situations.

Golden rules

1. Swap down
Exchange your pieces with enemy pieces until your opponent has virtually nothing left except king and pawns, and you still have fighting units.

2. Mop up
Use your extra pieces to clean up remaining enemy pieces.

3. Queen a pawn
Get a pawn to the end of the board. A new queen will make your checkmating task easy.

Endgame strategy

Good endgame play is the mark of a true master. Working out how to win without many pieces means that you will have to adopt a whole new strategy. Use the three golden rules in the box above.

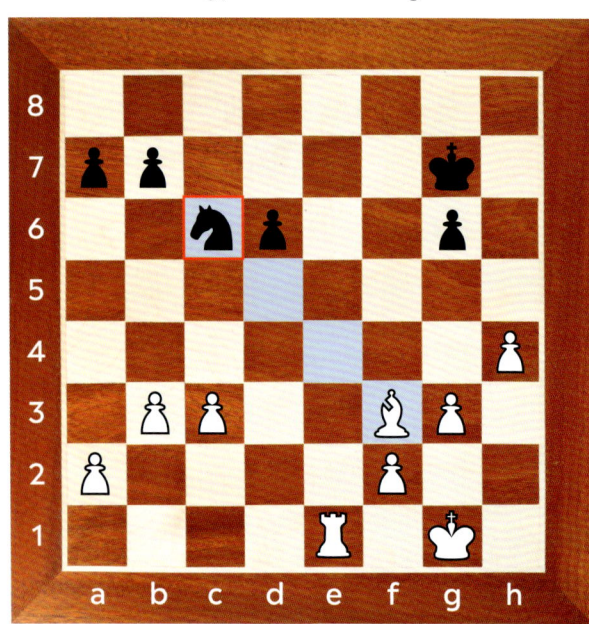

1.	Bxc6	bxc6
2.	Re7+	Kf6
3.	Rxa7	d5
4.	a4	

Black's pawn at a7 has been "mopped up".

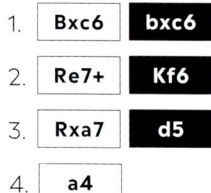

1 Look at this endgame. White is way ahead on points but is not going to be able to checkmate quickly, in particular because both queens are off the board. White starts by "swapping down". White's bishop takes the knight at c6, which will be recaptured by Black's pawn on b7. Follow the notation given here on your chess board to find out the rest of White's plan.

2 White has "swapped down", "mopped up", and with the move to a4 is now well on the way to "queening a pawn". It won't be long before White delivers checkmate.

It's your move!

Look at these two diagrams. Using the three golden rules – "swap down", "mop up", and "queen a pawn"– choose the correct moves to make in these endgame situations. (Answers on page 43.)

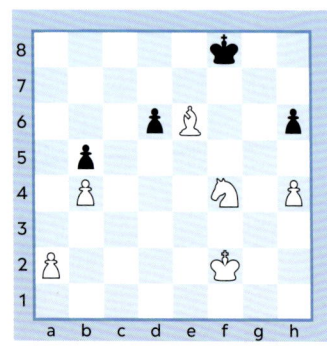

1 Which is the best move for White? Ng6+ or Bd7?

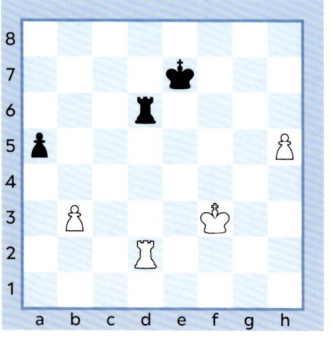

2 Should the white rook on d2 capture the black rook on d6 and then be recaptured? Or should White move the rook out of harm's way?

The lawn mower

We still haven't shown how to actually get checkmate with only a few pieces. The "lawn mower" makes a great weapon with which to crush your poor opponent. One army has two rooks and a king, against one king. Using the rooks as a team, it is possible to get checkmate very quickly.

1.	...
	Rg4

1 Set up your pieces in the position shown in this picture – Black's rooks on b7 and g8, Black's king on b8, and White's king on d3. Follow the moves on your board using the notation. Knowing that it would be difficult to give checkmate when the king is in the middle of the board, Black sets about driving the white king to the edge.

2.	**Kc3**	**Rh7**
3.	**Kd3**	**Rh3+**

2 Black gradually pushes the white king towards the edge. He is now stuck to the back three ranks of the board and will have to retreat further.

4.	**Ke2**	**Rg2+**
5.	**Kf1**	

3 The king is at last at the edge of the field and, by attacking the black rook, threatens to escape. But the slow-footed king is no match for the speedy rooks, who simply transfer themselves to the other side of the field.

5.	...	**Ra2**
6.	**Kg1**	**Rb3**
7.	**Kf1**	**Rb1#**

4 Black's rook moves forwards to b1 to give checkmate. The rooks have worked together to great effect. Study this checkmate carefully. It is called the "lawn mower" because the action of the rooks looks like someone mowing a lawn.

Other checkmates

It may be that you have even fewer pieces at your disposal. In fact with a king and a queen, or a king and a rook, you can still checkmate provided you use your king.

Queen mate
Here, White's king has played a vital role in the attack. Not only has he helped drive the black king to the edge, but also guards the queen as she delivers the kiss of death.

Box mate
This is called "Box mate" because the king and the rook work even more closely together than in Queen mate, and they gradually box in the enemy king.

It's a draw!

Sometimes players are so evenly matched that neither side is able to win and the game is a draw. There are several ways a game can be drawn, such as when neither player has enough strong pieces left, or a draw by agreement, when neither player can see a way to win. However, there are three other draws set out by the rule book. These are stalemate, a draw by repetition, and the 50-move rule.

Check it out!
In the 1993 World Championship match between reigning champion Gary Kasparov of Russia and Nigel Short of Great Britain, Kasparov was on the brink of defeat in two vital games. However, to stave off disaster, and to keep his championship title, he played a brilliant defence to get a draw in both games.

Stalemate

If a player cannot move any pieces, and their king, which is not in check, cannot move anywhere, the position is called a draw by stalemate. Here the black king cannot move except into check. He is not in check now so this game is a stalemate.

Not enough pieces
A situation may arise where you simply don't have enough strong pieces left to give checkmate. If only the two kings remain, they cannot checkmate each other. Likewise, you cannot give checkmate with only a bishop and king, or a knight and a king left. Without enough pieces a game results in a draw.

This is the best position that White can achieve with just a bishop and a king against a black king. It is impossible to get checkmate.

Forcing a stalemate

Sometimes it is worth intentionally bringing about a draw by stalemate, rather than losing. Here White, about to be checkmated, finds a cheeky way to draw.

The white rook moves across the board and puts the black king into check. Black is forced to capture the rook with the queen.

On the next move, White can't move any white pieces. The white king cannot move into check. Stalemate!

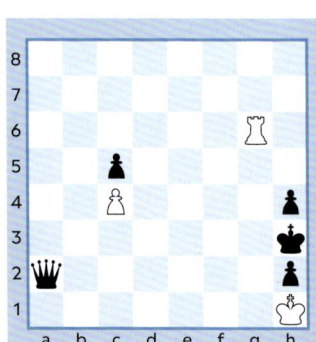

It's your move!
This is tricky! It is in White's interests to get a draw, otherwise Black will soon deliver checkmate. What move can White make with the rook on g6 to ensure that the result is a draw? Hint: disregard the queen. (Answer on page 43.)

Draw by repetition

If a position repeats itself three times, the game can be declared a draw. If one player keeps checking the other with no escape and no checkmate either, this is known as perpetual check. Look at this series of moves.

1 Black is in a bad postion. White has more points and two strong attacking pieces. Black decides to go for a draw by perpetual check. The black queen moves up to put the white king into check.

2 White has no other option but to move the king onto the edge to avoid check. However, the white king is not safe yet.

The white king is forced to move to the only safe square.

The 50-move rule

The third kind of draw in the chess rule book happens when no pawns have been moved and no captures have taken place for 50 moves. As you can imagine, this doesn't happen very often.

3 Black moves along the diagonal to deliver check again. The white king has nowhere to go unless he moves back to where he came from. The black queen will then move back to where she came from, putting the white king in check again. These moves could continue forever and the result of this game is a draw by perpetual check.

Taking it further

You can enjoy chess throughout your life, and it is up to you how you choose to play. Whether you prefer relaxing games with your friends at home or playing hard battles in tournaments, joining a chess club gets you off to a good start. The more you play, whether with your friends, at a chess club, online chess, against a computer, or in tournaments, the better you will be. So make your move and start playing!

Chess clubs

At chess clubs you can practise your skills and techniques against a variety of opponents, as well as get advice from a teacher. Some clubs may invite famous players to come and give talks and demonstrate their skills. Joining a school chess club has been the start for many top chess players! If you get into a school team, you can go to other schools to play matches. Playing against many different people will improve your game.

Tournaments

Entering a chess tournament means playing in more formal surroundings. At a tournament, you're not allowed any help from other people and your moves are timed.

The Mind Sports Olympiad

The Mind Sports Olympiad is the Olympics for all games that require mental agility. There are hundreds of games events, including backgammon, bridge, memory games, and speed-reading tests. Chess is an important part of the agenda. The Olympiad is held annually in England and anyone, from any country, can enter. Gold, silver, and bronze medals are awarded to the top juniors and top adults in each event.

Online chess

The internet is a great resource for chess players. There are many websites to choose from, and you can find opponents to play against all over the world.

Electronic chess

Electronic chess opponents come in many shapes and sizes, from super computers that take on grandmasters, to apps that can play against you. These are great for analysis, practice, and for when a human opponent is not available.

Young chess players
More than 600 young contestants from nine countries – Belarus, Estonia, Israel, Moldova, Poland, Portugal, Sweden, Switzerland, and Ukraine – take part in the First Vinnytsia International Golden Youth Cup, Vinnytsia, central Ukraine, 3 July 2019. At the time, the event set the national record for the largest children's chess tournament.

Glossary

During practice, or when watching a game, you may find it helpful to understand some of the following words and phrases.

B

Bishop A piece that only moves in a diagonal direction. Each army contains two bishops.

C

Capture When one piece takes an enemy piece. The capturing piece moves onto the square of the enemy piece, which is removed from the board.

Castling A special combined move where the king moves two squares towards a rook and the rook jumps over to stand next to the king.

Check An attack on a king.

Checkmate A situation in which a king is in check and cannot escape – therefore the end of the game.

Chess clock A double clock that measures the time taken by each player to make a move so that the game doesn't last too long.

D

Development Moving the pieces off the back row into a more central position in order to attack.

Diagonal The corner to far corner direction on the chess board.

Diagram A picture of a chess board with the chess pieces in place used to demonstrate specific positions.

Double attack *See* Fork.

Draw A game that cannot be won by either side.

E

Endgame The final phase of the game when only a few pieces are left.

En passant A move where a pawn that has moved up two squares on its initial move in the game can be captured by an enemy pawn standing alongside, as though the pawn had only moved one square.

Exchange A swap or trade of pieces.

F

File A straight column of squares going vertically – i.e. from one player to the other.

Fool's mate The shortest possible game ending in checkmate.

Fork When one piece attacks more than one enemy piece at the same time.

H

Half-open file A file with a pawn or pawns of only one colour on it.

I

Illegal move A move that breaks the rules of chess.

International Grandmaster A rank above the International Master. One of the strongest players in the world.

International Master A title for a chess player, recognizing internationally a player of great strength.

K

King The most important piece in the game. The whole aim of the game is to capture the enemy king.

King's side The files that are nearest the king – the f-, g-, and h-files, and sometimes the e-file is also included.

Knight The only piece that does not move in a straight line; the two knights on each side jump in an L-shape.

M

Mate Abbreviation for checkmate.

Material All the pieces and pawns on the board, apart from the king.

Middlegame The phase of the game between the opening and the endgame.

N

Notation The method of recording the moves of a game.

O

Open file A file on which there are no pawns of either colour.

Opening The first phase of the game; when the pieces are brought into position before the start of any attack.

P

Pawn The footsoldier of the chess board. Each army has eight pawns.

Perpetual check An endless series of checks that leads to a draw.

Piece In general, a member of the chess army. Sometimes used in the context of a piece meaning a king, queen, bishop, knight, or rook, as opposed to a pawn.

Pin An attack on a piece which, if it should move, leaves a more valuable piece open to capture.

Promotion Where a pawn becomes a queen, knight, rook, or bishop when it reaches the end of the board.

Q

Queen (noun) The most powerful piece on the board. Each army has one queen and she can move in either a horizontal, vertical, or diagonal direction.

Queen (verb) To promote a pawn to a queen.

Queen's side The files that are nearest the queen – the a-, b-, and c-files, and sometimes the d-file is also included.

R

Rank A straight row of squares going horizontally from one side of the board to the other.

Rook Each army has two rooks, which resemble castle towers. They move in a straight line along the ranks and files.

S

Sacrifice To give up material in order to fend off an attack or to gain advantage.

Scholar's mate A four-move checkmate, which can occur quite often between beginners.

Score The written record in notation of the moves of a game, usually on a score sheet.

Stalemate A position in which a king is not in check but the player has no legal move. Such a position is a draw.

Strategy The planning of long-term moves in a game rather than short-term tactics and actions.

T

Tactics The art of the double or multiple threat.

Answers

Page 13: Simple notation
White: Queen is on c1
Bishop is on g2
Pawn is on d4
Black: King is on e8
Knight is on b6
Rook is on h5

Page 14: Pawns
White pawns can capture the knight on d4, the bishop on b4, and the pawn on e5

Page 16: Bishops
The bishop moves in either of the following orders:
f6, d8, b6, a5, c3, e1, f2, g3
or f6, d8, b6, f2, g3, e1, c3, a5

Page 17: Knights
The knight jumps in either of the following orders:
d6, f5, g7, e6, d8, f7
or d6, f7, d8, e6, g7, f5

Page 18: Rooks
The rook moves in the following order:
f5, f3, g3, h3, h7, f7, d7, b7, b4

Page 21: King
1. White's rook moves to h8 to give checkmate

2. White's bishop moves to d5 to give checkmate

3. White's queen moves to c7 to give checkmate

Page 25: Further notation
1. The four moves are written as follows:
bxa3, Nxg1, g5, and Bd6+

Page 27: Opening
1a. Pawn to e4: good move
b. Pawn to h4: bad move because it puts a pawn on the edge
c. Knight to h3: not good – you move out a knight (Rule 2) but you put it on the edge
2a. Bishop to b5: bad move – you've already moved the bishop once
b. Knight to a3: bad move. Again, you moved out a knight, but put it on the edge.
c. Pawn to d3: good move. It puts a pawn in the centre and releases the bishop at c1.

3a. Knight to f3: bad move. You get a knight near the centre (Rule 2) but you lose your pawn at e4, which is threatened by the black bishop at b7. Guard your pieces! (Rule 4)
b. Pawn to e5: not good! Only move each piece once. (Rule 3)

c. Knight moves to c3: good choice! You get out a new piece (Rule 2) and you also defend your pawn at e4. (Rule 4)

Page 31: Key techniques
1. White can make the following captures:
Kxe3 (1 point), Kxf3 (3 points), Kxg3 (3 points), bxa6 (3 points), Nxf6 (5 points), Bxg8 (9 points – the best capture)

2. Qxf5 – not good as Black can recapture with a pawn, and White will lose the queen
gxh4 – good move because Black can only recapture a pawn, and White has won a bishop
Rxc7 – an equal exchange as Black can recapture your rook with the black rook on h7
Bxf8 – White wins Black's queen. Black's king will recapture White's bishop but the profit for White is 6 points. This is therefore the best capture for White.

3. The ten safe moves for White are: Re1, Qg1, Kg1, Rc3, Ra1, Na1, Qe1, Ke1, h4, Bb5

4. Rd4 – safe
Bxc7 – not safe
Rd7 – safe enough
Be5 – safe enough

Page 32: Attack and defend
1. White can make the following threats:
Bb6 attacking the rook at d8
Rc7 attacking the pawn on b7
Rg1 attacking the queen on g7
Bh4 attacking the rook on d8
2. The seven threatening moves are:
Qf7 attacks the bishop at e7
Nf5 also attacks the bishop at e7
Rd5 attacks the queen at c5
Ne4 also attacks the queen at c5
Qf3 attacks the rook at a8
Bd5 also attacks the rook at a8
c4 attacks the knight at b5
If you found them all, congratulations!

Page 33: Attack and defend (continued)
1. Support: Kg2, Kh2, Rc3
Counter-attack: Rc7 attacks the knight at b7, Rc8+ attacks the king at g8
Move: Ng5 moves the knight to a safe-enough square

2. Move: Qe2, Qe1, Qb6
Block: f4
Counter-attack: also f4, attacks both the knight at e5 and the bishop at g5; Bd5+ attacks the king at g8

Page 36: Endgame
1. The best move for White is Bd7, as next move the bishop can "mop up" the pawn at b5 and go on to "queen a pawn", ensuring victory.

2. Yes, White should capture the rook and then be recaptured ("swap down"). White will then be able to "queen a pawn" on the h-file.

Page 38: It's a draw!
Rg3. Black's next move must be to capture the rook, which has the king in check. White can then not move the king – stalemate!

Index

Useful addresses

The English Chess Federation
The Watch Oak
Chain Lane
Battle
East Sussex TN33 0YD
Tel: 01424 775222
email: office@englishchess.org.uk
Website: www.englishchess.org.uk

Australian Chess Federation Inc
22 Bruarong Crescent,
Frankston South,
Victoria 3199
Australia
Tel: 0409 525 963
email: president@auschess.org.au
Website: auschess.org.au

NSW Chess Association
GPO Box 2418
Sydney NSW 2001
Australia
Tel: 02 9498 2760
Website: www.nswca.org.au

FIDE (Fédération Internationale des Échecs)
54, Avenue de Rhodanie
1007, Lausanne,
Switzerland
Tel: 0041 21 6010039
Website: www.fide.com

UK Chess Challenge
Westminster House,
10 Westminster Road, Macclesfield
Cheshire SK10 1BX
United Kingdom
Tel: 07776 455144
email: admin@ukchess.co.uk
Website: delanceyukschoolschesschallenge.com

Useful websites

General links:
www.chess.com

Playing chess online:
www.chessclub.com

Chess chat:
chess.co.uk
www.chesscafe.com

Kasparov website:
https://www.kasparov.com

Chess Scotland:
www.chessscotland.com

Chess lessons:
www.chesscorner.com

Mind Sports Olympiad:
https://msoworld.com

Australian chess:
www.auschess.org.au

New Zealand chess:
www.newzealandchess.co.nz

Acknowledgments

The publisher would like to thank the following people for their help with making the book:
Caroline Greene, Amanda Rayner, Lee Simmons, and Penny York for editorial assistance; Jacqueline Gooden, Tory Gordon-Harris, Rebecca Johns, and Tassy King for design assistance; Manpreet Kaur and Deepak Negi for picture research; Mrinmoy Mazumdar for DTP assistance; Saloni Singh for the jacket; Hazel Beynon for proofreading; and Hilary Bird for the index.

The publisher would like to thank the following for their kind permission to reproduce their photographs:
(Key: a-above; b-below/bottom; c-centre; f-far; l-left; r-right; t-top)

AKG London: 22tr. **Alamy Stock Photo:** CPA Media Pte Ltd / Pictures From History 8-9c; Artepics 9bc; XiXinXing 9cb. **Bridgeman Art Library, London/ New York:** 12tr, 20tr. **Dreamstime.com:** Gresei (chess board) 0-45; Carlos Soler Martinez 18tr. **Getty Images:** Alisdair MacDonald / Mirrorpix 38tr. **Mary Evans Picture Library:** 14tr. **Hulton Getty:** 24tr.

All other images © Dorling Kindersley